M000028683

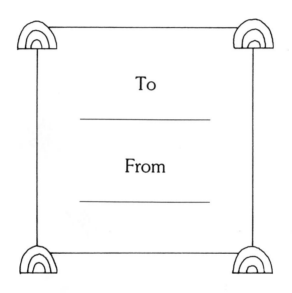

To

_____

From

_____

OTHER BOOKS BY DAVID HELLER

Children on
Happiness

Children on Happiness

*Happiness Is a Tickle in Your Heart
and a Smile on Your Face*

David Heller

Villard Books  New York 1994

All rights reserved under International and Pan-American
Copyright Conventions. Published in the United States by
Villard Books, a division of Random House, Inc., New York,
and simultaneously in Canada by Random House of Canada
Limited, Toronto.

Villard Books is a registered trademark of Random House, Inc.

Library of Congress Cataloging-in-Publication Data
Heller, David.
Children on happiness: happiness is a tickle in your heart
and a smile on your face/by David Heller.
p.   cm.
ISBN 0-679-43039-3
1. Happiness in children—Quotations, maxims, etc.
2. Happiness—Quotations, maxims, etc.   3.Cheerfulness—
Quotations, maxims, etc.
I. Title.
BF723.H37H45   1994
170—dc20   94-7175

Manufactured in the United States of America on acid-free paper.

3   5   7   9   8   6   4   2

First Edition

To all the children I have
interviewed over the years,
and to our own children
yet to come

"We find delight in the beauty and happiness
of children, that makes the heart too big
for the body."
—EMERSON

Introduction

We are all participants in the pursuit of happiness. In one form or another, we ask ourselves "What will make me happy?" Naturally, there are as many answers to the question as there are people in the world. Every great mind has contributed his or her two cents on the subject, but we still aren't all that definitive about what makes a person happy. Perhaps children, with their eyes always so wide open, may offer us a fresh outlook on the subject. Nurtured by the experiences of the second grade and the playground, youngsters express some prevailing views with great homespun wisdom and build on existing notions with playful originality.

"Happiness is the calm, glad, certainty of innocence," wrote the playwright Henrik Ibsen. Indeed, the innocence of children provides them with a unique perspective on how to be happy. Children see the world through the lens of initial discovery. In their world, every day is a fresh opportunity to explore and discover. So they seek out happiness in the novel and elemental preoccupations of childhood—at play, in the classroom, at the dinner table, or in the family living room where conversations about life routinely take place. They suggest that these are good places to search for happiness and to understand how to master it.

"Happiness is there for all," thought Mark Twain, "but most of us look the other way and lose it." Children may well be our guides to happiness, put here on this earth to help us remember how to set our sights. Armed with Frisbees and water pistols and born with a taste for cotton candy, kids are ever prepared, Tom Sawyer-style, to bring a little joy and frolic into the world—as long as the adults around don't interfere. Youngsters are always importuning us to join in their merry festivities, as if directing us toward fun (theme parks, here we come). And if we seem to be looking in a different direction, children are mystified that we can't spot happiness quite as clearly and definitely as they do.

"Love is the master key that opens the gates of happiness," observed Oliver Wendell Holmes, Jr. Now youngsters will tell that this Wendell fellow knew what he was talking about, for the importance of close relationships with regard to happiness is not lost on them. Many of the children's first associations to cheering up bring mention of Mom or Dad, a special friend or a brother or sister. These little philosophers intuitively understand that happiness is not a feeling which stands in isolation but an emotion that is most often accompanied by love, friendliness, camaraderie, or just plain goodwill.

In this collection of quotations, a large gathering of youngsters talk about what makes them happy and what might help others to be happy too. The children are freewheeling with their advice and yet respectful of the idea that everyone must find his or her own route to happiness. After all, the children reason, some kids prefer skateboarding and others like roller-skating. When it comes to happiness, there's no disputing matters of taste! But the crucial thing—the children seem to be saying—is to keep rolling along and refuse to quit. Happiness may well be just around the corner as long as you keep heading toward it.

—DAVID HELLER, Ph.D.

Children on
Happiness

What Is Happiness?

"It's having a gigantic Pez dispenser in
your bedroom."
Vincent, age 8

"Happiness is a tickle in your heart and a
smile on your face."
Leslie, age 9

"Happiness is just having a good feeling about yourself."
Mitchell, age 10

"It's when it snows so much that the man on the radio says the magic words: *'no school.'* "
Alexander, age 8

"Happiness is having somebody to share your swing set with."
Crystal, age 7

"It's having two quarters in your pocket when you thought you only had one."
Carlos, age 9

"Happiness is even better than fudge."
Cara, age 7

"Happiness is like a hamburger because it goes with everything and it feels good when it's inside you."
Omar, age 8

"Happiness is what people want, but I sure wish there was directions about how to get it."
Ryan, age 9

"Happiness is like a tree because it has many roots."
Maria, age 9

The Inner Experience: What Does It Feel Like to Be Happy?

"Like you are flying like an eagle, but you still feel pretty as a dove."
Trisha, age 10

"You feel like you want to skip."
Julie, age 6

"It's something like tasting watermelon, only better. . . . There isn't any pits to worry about."

Carlos, age 9

"Happiness feels like you are winning an Oscar award, even though you have only been in three plays at school."

Helene, age 9

"You feel pretty free. . . . Happiness usually comes when you don't have any homework."

Lisa, age 10

"Happiness feels like you have all kinds of
bright colors inside you."
Nina, age 9

What Is the Cause of Most People's Troubles in Life?

"Having to erase . . . Mistakes are no fun."
Afton, age 7

"Too many worries, not enough skeet ball."
Jason, age 9

"Being left-handed in a right-handed world."
Todd, age 10

"For women, it's usually men."
Eleanor, age 8

"Serious problems with being dull . . . Many grown-ups are too afraid to take chances."
Alana, age 8

"Not enough hugs from Mom."
Thomas, age 8

"Ugliness . . . not so much the kind on the outside, but more the kind on the inside that makes people mean."
Ellen, age 9

Wise Things to Remember
When You Are a Little Down

"Rain always makes way for sunshine."
Mark, age 10

"You may not have all the answers in life, but cheer
up, at least you know how to read already."
Vivian, age 8

"Say to yourself: 'Troubles, troubles go away . . .
work yourself out another way.' "
Sammie, age 9

"Sadness isn't real popular with other people either,
so maybe it won't stay in the world that long."
Kelly, age 9

"Think about the people you love and the people
who love you. . . . That will always help."
Carey, age 8

Putting Wisdom into Action: Basic Things You Can Do to Cheer Up and Put a Touch of Joy in Your Life

"Put a red ribbon in your hair. . . . Boys better not do it or they're asking for trouble."

Lori, age 7

"Sing 'I Love Me' to yourself . . . but not too loud. People might start to wonder about you."

Kenny, age 8

"Tease your father."

Megen, age 8

"Find a person to read a story to you. . . . Stories are good because they let you dream about pirates and dragons and that might make you feel better."

William, age 6

"Make sure you have some quiet time every day. . . . You should remember that even great people like George Washington took naps when he wasn't busy with a revolution."

Isaac, age 9

More Advanced Things That Could Make Even the Saddest Person in the World Cheer Up

"If Disneyworld moved right next door to you."
Aliya, age 4

"If Saturday and Sunday were the only days adults worked and they had the rest of the week off."
Steve, age 10

"If you could use leaves instead of money to buy things . . . then you'd have a double reason to be happy when the leaves start falling off the trees."

Camille, age 10

"If dolls could talk and tell you how beautiful you are."

Melissa, age 6

"If war was just ancient history and we could all get along."

John, age 8

"If there was no dying, but when people got old and tired they just went for a rest somewhere like Bermuda."

Amanda, age 8

The List of Happiness No-Nos: These Things Will Definitely Keep You from Being Happy

"Nightmares about giant reptiles."
Denny, age 9

"Letting your dad know that you are questioning his authority . . . *big mistake.*"
Elvin, age 9

"Saying stuff like 'What difference does it make?' . . . You should feel like everybody can make a difference."

Denise, age 11

"Problems with your cable connection."

Graham, age 9

"Like if the sun is out and everybody else is saying it's a great day. But you are the kind of person who looks at it and says that it's no big deal, because it will probably rain all next weekend."

Gene, age 9

Personal Revelations:
When You Are a Bit Sad,
What Cheers *You* Up?

"Onion rings . . . Once it's in a ring, those
onions don't make you cry. They make your
taste buds smile."
Chris, age 10

"Upbeat rap music that says: 'Hey, man, why so
low? Hey, man, I'm your friend, not your foe.'"
Isaac, age 9

"Looking at the books in the children's part of the bookstore cheers me up. There're more good drawings there than you can see in an art museum."

Ellen, age 9

"I lie down in the middle of a pile of leaves and pretend I'm the prettiest leaf of all."

Ginger, age 8

"I watch sports with my father and he explains the rules and we act like men together."

Oscar, age 8

"I get cheered up by both candy and people. . . . Both of them help me because both of them can be pretty sweet if you pick the right one."

Lottie, age 6

"I go outside and see how the bugs and the birds aren't sad, so why should I be?"

Eleanor, age 8

More Personal Revelations:
Who Cheers You Up?

"My grandmother . . . She makes the best corn chowder, and corn chowder is good cheer-up food in winter."

Jason, age 9

"My dog, Bruce. He's always optimistic."

Seth, age 10

"I used to get cheered up by Big Bird, but
then he got to be just a bunch of feathers. . . .
Now I like Seinfeld."

Thomas, age 8

"Anybody who gives me an allowance."

Denny, age 9

"Clowns . . . I don't believe their sad faces because I
know clowns have a job to do."

Kevin, age 7

"My mother and my father and my grandmas . . .
They are all really good at cheering up and I
cheer them up too."

Carey, age 8

The Advice the Children Give to Their Own Young Friends About How to Cheer Up and Be Happier

"Don't worry, you can be happy just like me. The secret is to do hardly any homework."
Elliot, age 10

"Head troubles are bad for you . . . but sometimes if you wear your favorite baseball cap your head might feel better.
Cory, age 6

"Don't argue with your parents, M.J. . . . Those parents will find a way to win every time. Trust me, I know about these things."

Sybil, age 9

"Don't be sad, Waldo. It's not your fault your parents named you bad."

Jason, age 9

Happiness Is the Natural Order of Things: What Can We Learn About Cheering Up and Being Happy From the Animal Kingdom?

"Cats prove that you can be happy just by getting fed without having to work hard for it."

Jason, age 9

"You should do what a sad dog does if you are feeling bad—find a shady tree to camp out under."

John, age 8

"Flying with freedom is a big part of happiness. . . . Birds are
real lucky creatures."
Laura, age 10

"Happiness is not having any worries or cares, just like a monkey. . . . Of course, that all could change if some other monkey takes his banana away."

Daniel, age 10

"It's not good to think about being part of the food chain if you want to get cheered up. . . . Tuna probably have a lot of worry problems."

Ryan, age 9

"Chickens probably know the most about happiness. . . . Sometimes happiness is just being able to lay eggs and feel like you produced something."

Sandra, age 11

Location, Location, Location!
What Are Some of the Best Places to Seek Happiness?

"In a toy store . . . That's a can't-miss place
for happiness."
Carey, age 8

"In a fully stocked refrigerator . . . What can I say for
myself, I'm not big on diets."
Chris, age 10

"In a hotel that has a swimming pool, a Jacuzzi, and the Cartoon Channel."
Michael J., age 7

"I would say at water parks and miniature golf courses."
Paul, age 8

"In your pocket . . . especially if you have a big one that can fit a picture of your whole family."
Elizabeth, age 9

"Look into the past and the future and see what happiness you can find there. But if you can't find it in the *now* time, then you probably aren't going to be happy."
Alice, age 9

"I seek happiness when I look up at the sky and try to figure out who is up there."
Bernadette, age 8

Being a Happiness Detective: How Can You Tell If a Person Is Really Happy?

"Tickle them and see how strong their laugh is."
Natalie, age 7

"They're supposed to have pink on their cheeks from smiling so much."
Marie, age 6

"Get up close and count their worry lines. . . . More than seven is bad news."

Jack, age 8

"A person singing 'Pop Goes the Weasel' is definitely happy."

Jeremy, age 8

"Ask the man if he has the time. If he says time isn't important, then he's probably a happy person."

Miles, age 11

"Smart people are happy because they are smart enough to know that being down-in-the-dumps is a colossal waste of time."

Mike P., age 10

"Happy people are the ones who believe that most things in life work out for the best."

Denise, age 11

"Show me a grown-up who likes to give kids a ride on his shoulders and I'll show you a happy grown-up."

Ben, age 8

Those Happy-Go-Lucky Folks We Know: Who Is the Happiest Person that You Can Think of?

"Pretty much any angel . . . because they already
got to where they want to go."

Carlos, age 9

"My mother . . . She spends a lot of her free time
with gingerbread men and then we eat them up to
make room for the next shift."

Ben, age 8

"Policemen . . . They got the best uniforms and they don't even have to pay for them."
Bert, age 7

"It's probably somebody in the third grade. They get to stay out longer for recess."
Guy, age 7

"People who make blankets are happy, because they know that they are keeping other people warm."
Noni, age 9

The Necessary Elements of a Run-of-the-Mill Happy Day for People Like You and Me

"Running outside with your pet . . . unless it's your turtle because that would be too dangerous for him."

Al H., age 8

"I'd have to say that it would have to include seeing God up close."

Carlos, age 9

"Sunshine and maybe just a few clouds for variety."
Bob, age 8

"Television with all the commercials taken out."
Cammy, age 8

"A day where the kids tell the parents what chores to do."
Ben, age 8

"A day with enough snow to go around the whole world. That way you could go sledding from one country to another."
Harold, age 7

What Three Grown-up Things Will You Absolutely Require in the Future to Insure Your Personal Happiness?

"Three more inches so I can make the basketball team."
Mario, age 11

"Larry, Mo, and Curly . . . You got to watch the *Three Stooges* on Saturday mornings."
Larry, age 10

"Money, a house, and a license to be a secret agent."
Ernie, age 8

"Three months off school at Christmas."
Ryan, age 9

"Visiting my grandma every week, being good at writing stories, and having a Snickers bar after dinner every night."
Caroline, age 7

"The three most important things are being healthy and being happy and being there for the people you care about."
Pam, age 10

The Icing on the Cake: What Not-So-Vital Thing Would Make You the Happiest Person Alive?

"A ring like my mother's."
Aliya, age 4

"I wouldn't want to be a millionaire. I don't need those kind of headaches. I just want to be an acrobat."
Mike K., age 8

"An elephant who lives in my backyard would make me the happiest person alive. He could use his trunk to get my ball when it goes over the fence."

Ben, age 8

"A screen test to replace that *Home Alone* kid when he retires."
Mario, age 11

"Changing into a faster runner, instead of the average-speed person that I am."
Marty, age 8

"I already have what makes me the happiest . . . my little sister."
Carey, age 8

"Anytime I see a smile on my mama's face, that makes me the happiest person alive."
Charlene, age 7

Happiness and Money:
What Is the Relationship Between
Owning Things and Being Happy?

"Money doesn't buy happiness. It buys cars and
houses and bicycles, but those are good too."

Marcia, age 8

"I own a television but it mostly makes me happy
when I have somebody else to watch it with."

Adam, age 8

"It's good to collect things, but it's better to collect happiness."

Joyce, age 8

"Happiness isn't made of money; happiness is made of love."

Sean, age 10

Social Happiness:
What Does Being Happy Have to
Do With Being With Other People?

"Happiness comes when somebody else's heart
says hello to yours."
Bernadette, age 8

"Back rubs make me happy, and you need some
other person with strong hands to give you one."
Andre, age 9

"Teachers make you happy when they don't call on you when you don't know the answer."

Katie, age 9

"Your father can help you be happy by bringing home a surprise; you can make him happy by raking the leaves."

Al G., age 9

"Different people might make you laugh and have a good time, but you got to be happy on your own. . . . It's sort of a personal thing."

Judy, age 8

Prescriptions for a Happy Life
for Anyone Over Thirty:
Here Are the Doctor's Orders

"Take two candy bars and call me in the morning."
Bernadette, age 8

"Take a bath every night with Mr. Bubbles."
Kimberly, age 5

"Every morning, you should get up and immediately sing 'Row, Row, Row Your Boat.' . . . Then you'll feel better."

Drew, age 8

"Loosen up a bit, lounge around when you can, and make sure you take lots of nice calm naps in an air-conditioned place."

Carey, age 8

"Once a month, call in sick and take your kids to a museum. . . . It will be an education for the whole family."

Elizabeth, age 9

"Don't worry so much. I don't, and I don't have any marks on my face."

Joy, age 7

"Don't pretend to be happy when you aren't. That only works in Hollywood."

Josiah, age 8

"If you are lonely, you can always write somebody. . . . This message was sponsored by the United States Postal Service."

Lane, age 9

"Think of life as a bowl of cherries. . . . They aren't rotten unless you smoosh them."

Carlos, age 9

"Give somebody else a smile and the smile will come back toward you."

Austin, age 8

The One Philosophical Thing You Should Always Remember If You Want to Be Among the Fortunate Who Call Themselves Happy

"Don't squint. . . . Get glasses if you have to because the world is too beautiful a place for you not to see it."

Carlos, age 9

"Perfume can make you smell good, but only you can make you feel good."

Esther, age 9

"A person is happy if she can laugh about a fortune cookie, no matter what the fortune cookie says."
Tracey, age 11

"Life is worth living. . . . Take it from me. I'm eight, but I know that already."
Charles, age 8

"Happy people don't cry over spilled milk; they cry because of joy flowing out of them."
Lauren, age 11

"Happiness isn't exactly what other people say it is, so don't believe all of the rumors about it. Go by your own experience."

Courtney, age 10

"Every minute of the day is happier if it has some love in it."

Earl, age 8

"You can still be happy if you have a sore ankle, but you can't be happy if you have a sore heart."

Elvin, age 9

Is Happiness Temporary
or Can It Be Forever?

"I think it is forever but you get to remember that
stuff like annoying sisters can be forever too."
John, age 8

"Happiness is forever if you are willing to do
what it takes. . . . Brace yourself, it might mean
kissing a lot."
Ben, age 8

"Happiness is temporary if it's Labor Day weekend
and you have to start school on Tuesday."
Robbie, age 9

"It's a temporary thing if you are waiting around for
other people to make you happy. . . . You have to
get up and do it yourself, girl."
Denise, age 11

Sharing Happiness: When You're Feeling Happy, What Can You Do to Spread the Happiness Around?

"Tell nearby grown-ups that they are looking younger every day."
Ben, age 8

"Clap your hands. It might catch on."
Sybil, age 9

"Kiss people at a restaurant like Roy Rogers. Even ones you never met before."
Chandra, age 6

"If every kid is riding bikes and a kid in your neighborhood doesn't have one, let him ride yours for a while."
Brice, age 8

"Draw smiley faces on all the cards you give to people."
Bernadette, age 8

"The biggest thing might be to try to have a kind
word for everyone you meet."
Sean, age 10

"Run for class officer at school and say that you are
a member of the Happiness Party."
Trisha, age 10

Happiness Worldwide: What Makes People All Over the Globe Happy?

"Seeing people in love."
Maria, age 9

"Americans spending money in their countries."
Miles, age 11

"Clear skies and no armies."
Eleanor, age 8

"The first good beach day."
Kera, age 9

"Hamsters who smile at you."
Robert, age 5

"The sound of children laughing."
Mindy, age 8

"Cars with people in them that aren't in a hurry."
Omar, age 8

"Rainbows."
Leah, age 9

"Being part of the human family."
Michael Y., age 10

Reflections on the Secret of Happiness

"The secret of happiness is learning how to say
'Have a nice day' and really meaning it."
Carol, age 9

"It's being grateful for your parents and it's them
being grateful for you."
Eleanor, age 8

"It is smelling flowers in the spring and remembering what they smell like in the winter."
Denise, age 11

"The secret is not wishing that you were more grown-up. . . . It's just being the kid you are."
Elizabeth, age 9

"Try to go toward happiness; don't go away from it."
Carey, age 8

"Collect love everywhere you go."
Jasmine, age 9

"It's being happy with who you are. . . . There isn't anybody else exactly like you who has the same chance at happiness that you do."

Doreen, age 11

"Live each day like it's something you should treasure; don't just act like you are killing time here on this earth."

Devon, age 11

"Remember that your happiness shouldn't depend on what it's like outside; happiness depends on what you feel on the inside."

Belinda, age 11

"The secret of happiness is kindness . . . not just toward other people but being kind to yourself too."

Michael Y., age 10

DAVID HELLER, Ph.D., is the author of fifteen previous books including *Just Build the Ark and the Animals Will Come: Children on Bible Stories, Dear God: Children's Letters to God, Love Is Like a Crayon Because It Comes in All Colors,* and *My Mother Is the Best Gift I Ever Got.* Additional books include *The Best Christmas Presents Are Wrapped in Heaven* and *Grandparents Are Made for Hugging.*

Dr. Heller's books about children have been selected three times by the Literary Guild, by the Book-of-the-Month Club, Quality Paperback Book Club, the Doubleday Book Club, and several others. His work has been featured on *20/20* and in *Parents* magazine, *People, Parenting, Cosmopolitan, Good Housekeeping, Catholic Digest, Woman's Day, Redbook, New Woman,* and many other periodicals. His books have been published in ten different foreign versions.

Dr. Heller lives in Boston with his wife and collaborator, Elizabeth.